In The Know

Setting Up Your Child For
The STEM World

A guide to help get your child into science, technology, engineering, and math

SECOND EDITION

CaT Bobino, M.S.

facebook.com/InTheKnowConsulting

@InTheKnowShow

@InTheKnowConsulting

i

For my parents —
my mom for putting me into everything she
could find and my dad for paying for it!

Thank you to:

Mom & Dad
Shalia
Elan
Banea
Chanelle

And everyone who has believed in me from day one!

Contents

PREFACE

Thank you for taking the time to purchase this book. The basis behind this is to give you suggestions and guidance that may help your child or student want to go into the Science, Technology, Engineering and Mathematics (STEM) field, while integrating personal experiences. STEM careers offer a variety of opportunities with job security and growth. This book is not a guarantee that he/she will even want to go into Science, Technology, Engineering, or Math, but it can help open their eyes to the possibilities that awaits them in the field.

There are so many facets to Science, Technology, Engineering, and Math. There are multiple options that allow people to shape their pathways and their career. Over the course of two years, I have met multiple people throughout STEM that have discussed the paths they took, their ups and downs, their highs and the lows, and the ultimate outcomes of their journey. For me to say that everyone ended on a positive note or that everyone was happy throughout the journey would be a fabrication of truth. Just as in any other field, there are bumps in the road and unexpected forks and dead ends. But that does not mean your journey has ended, only that a new journey has begun.

This book should be used as a tool to help you guide your child or your student through school while focusing on STEM related careers, but it can also be a guide for yourself. On the pages that asks you to make outlines or to fill in the blanks, fill it in for yourself too. If you want to embark on a personal journey to understand and/or work in STEM, then this book is for you as well. Along the way, I added in some personal journeys that I took as well as the biggest influences in my life. What you may not know or even fully understand is that you are the biggest influence in your child's life, or you could be the biggest influence in your student's life, but it takes determination, time, and effort.

I firmly believe that it takes a village to raise a child. That does not mean you bring in every neighbor, every teacher, or even every family member to help raise a child. Yet, it means that you cannot do it alone.

Allow yourself to ask for help, or to be a helping hand. If you see that a child needs more than you can offer, then find someone that may be able to offer what you can't. Asking for help does not make you weak, nor does it make you incapable, it actually makes you much smarter than the person that did not ask for help. It means you know your limitations and that you acknowledge them. Furthermore, it means you know what you can do for your child or your student and how far you can take them.

So my question to you is: How far are you willing to go?

Chapter 1

READING IS FUNDAMENTAL

Reading is seriously fundamental. It is important to start reading to your child in the very beginning. Around the 18th week of pregnancy, your baby will be able to hear sounds. You can start practicing reading aloud to your child then. This is just practice, for although your child can hear you, they are only hearing sounds. Once you give birth to the age of 3, your child's brain triples in size! As they grow, they learn how to communicate with you by your reactions to what they do, like when they cry, fuss, make bubbles, or even smile. They are learning critical ways to communicate, and when they are spoken to, they hear words consistently being said and may learn these words faster. Studies have shown that if a child comes from a talkative family, they did better on cognitive tests.

This is just a way of saying your child may do better in school if they are talked to while their brain is developing. As they start to recognize colors, shapes, or even words, allow them to read along with you. Take their fingers over each word as you pronounce them, allowing them to make connections with what they see and what they hear. Buy them their own children's books that you can read repeatedly (caution, you WILL get tired of the book, but think of the child!) The younger you do this, the more willing they are to read on their own and have a passion for reading. This is important, for as they get older, they will have to read a lot in Science, Technology, Engineering, and even Math (STEM).

List Of Books That You Have In Your House

_____

_____

_____

_____

_____

_____

_____

_____

_____

_____

_____

_____

_____

_____

_____

_____

_____

_____

_____

_____

_____

_____

_____

Books You Have For Your Infant/Toddler

_____

_____

_____

_____

_____

_____

_____

_____

_____

_____

_____

_____

_____

_____

_____

_____

_____

_____

_____

_____

_____

_____

_____

_____

My earliest nerdy memory of elementary school was in the first grade. Back then, many moons ago, when you were in the first grade, you didn't have to stay the entire day. In fact, the first graders where broken up into two different groups – the first group got there early, just like the rest of the kids. They started the day around 8:30, and ended the day around 1:30. I was a part of the group that started school a little later. This was because I could read at an accelerated level, and any students that could do this, went to a special after school program.

I got to school around 9:30, and fell in line with the rest of the first graders after their first recess (remember recess? It was great!). After arriving at the time of recess, we would start the class where the rest of the students had finished, and we did the same work. When class was over at 1:30, the first to arrive students went home, while the rest of us were asked to read books for an hour. Our teacher would discuss some of the books with us, but mostly, we read. And I loved to read. At that time, my favorite books where the Bernstein Bears. I started a collection from the book order forms that spanned for many years. In fact, my mother still has some of those books in her garage. Remember those order forms? I also loved any book that taught me about animals. I would want to order 5, 6, 7 books at a time. My parents couldn't afford to buy all the books that I wanted, so I had to settle for library books instead. My mother cultivated my love for books. She would take me to Dimond Library in Oakland, where I always walked out with a collection of books. As I got older, and started going to the public library, I started reading Ranger Rick books, as well as Garfield, and Ren Tin Tin.

Books were fascinating to me. I could get lost in a story and read books for hours. I would take books with me and read them everywhere: in the car, at the grocery store, at the dinner table, and in my room. As I got older, I got the nickname 'hermit' because I would be in my room for hours reading, and my family would not see me (nor did them miss me!).

Towards the end of elementary school, I started reading the Goose Bump series. I remember reading Super Fudge, Are You There God; It's Me Margaret, If You Give A Mouse A Cookie, The Magic School Bus, and many more. When I was growing up, there was a wonderful program on television called Reading Rainbow. I loved that show, because it reaffirmed what I already knew, that I could go anywhere, anytime, and anyplace with the help of a book. I would sit down and listen to all the titles that they would read off, and see if I could find those books myself. Reading came natural to me.

Now consider your reading activities when you were younger. What did you like to read? What drew in your attention? If your student or child is open to the idea of reading, foster it. Help them identify books that they may enjoy, and even open their minds to authors they may not have known about. Reading opens the door to being creative and open minded, and that can correlate to being open minded and creative when solving problems in Science, Technology, Engineering, and Math.

List Of Books That Are Good For Elementary Aged Kids

_____

_____

_____

_____

_____

_____

_____

_____

_____

_____

_____

_____

_____

_____

_____

_____

_____

_____

_____

_____

_____

_____

_____

_____

_____

_____

When you teach your children the benefits of reading, they will take it with them throughout life. They will find any reason to curl up with a good book. It is important for them to learn this because having a love of reading, or even having a tolerance to reading will help get them through high school and college. For me, I have never been truly fond of reading scientific journals or reports. I think they can go on and on and all I need to know is the experiment, results, and conclusion. When I went to undergraduate school, I had to read lots of journal entries for my classes. My love of long novels helped my tolerance of long journals. Through reading at elementary, middle, and high school, I learned to make it through college.

A distinct memory that I have is from the eighth grade at Montera Middle School; or Montera Junior High School while I was a student there. I was in English class, and we were having silent reading time. I did not have anything to read for I had already finished my book, so I went to the back of the class and looked around our very meager book rack. I picked up a book that had an interesting name and decided to read it. It was a good book and it only took me a few days to finish it. A few months later, the teacher announced that she was picking a book for us all to read and write a report about. When she said the name of the book, I chuckled inwardly. I had to write a book report about an adolescent coming into his own. I already knew the story because I had read it a few months prior – it was The Catcher in the Rye. Score one for the nerdy girl that just likes to read.

Another memory about reading that catapults me to high school, was my junior year at Encinal High School. In our class, we had to read The Great Gatsby. After a few chapters, the teacher administered a test about the book. I, sitting directly in the middle of the class, had my shoulder tapped quite a few times to answer questions about the book during the test. One student had the audacity to ask me the NAME of the main female character! Although I was taken aback by the fact that this student didn't even read the first few pages to find out the name of the character, I whispered as best as I could that the name was Daisy. I believe he was the ring leader of the cheaters, and also could not hear very well, for a number of students had wrote the name wrong. These were all students that had sat around me and that particular student. I don't know what name they wrote, or how the teacher found out it was me that they were trying to cheat off of, but the next time we had a test, the teacher separated me from the rest of the class. I had to sit at a desk in front of the class away from everyone. If I didn't feel like a nerd before, I certainly did then.

List Of Books For Middle And High School

When I got to college, I will not lie, my reading took a bit of a nose dive. Here goes a sheltered girl from Oakland, California now living in Tuscaloosa, Alabama with no one watching over her shoulder and making rules. In fact, there were no rules. I lived in the Honors dorm, which mean I could come and go as I pleased because we all had a key to the front door. No one made us check in or out, and I had freedom that I never knew existed before. It wasn't quite like Hillman from A Different World, but it was an HBCU where I made lasting friendships and got to dive into my major, Biology.

Since I was majoring in Biology, and because I was there on full scholarship under the Harte Honors program, I was expected to take my major classes as well as honor classes. By the time my biology, chemistry, math, English, history, language, and religion classes all added up, I was around 21 credits a semester. Although I have 3 siblings that went to college before me, and college educated parents, this was my first experience with college enrollment. My classes where already predetermined by my major and by my scholarship, so I thought it was normal to have 21 credits. It wasn't until my junior year at Stillman College when one of my friends was telling me how they were taking 12 units and was considered full time. I didn't understand. How can you only take 12 units and be full time? Do you not have to do more than that? I asked a few more people, and they all gave me the same story – 12 units was all you needed to be considered full time. So, why was I taking 21 units? By then, it did not matter. I had above a 3.0 in my classes and still have enough time to go out and party with friends, while running for the track team. In fact, I wondered why people didn't take more units so that they would be done with school, since it was so easy to handle that many classes at once.

By the time I went into my senior year at Stillman, I only had one class to take – biochemistry. That class was a beast taught by a beast of a woman. She was a small, older woman who didn't understand if you didn't get the answer to the questions right away. When you asked her to explain something, she would look at you like you was born yesterday, for the answer was right there in the book, and she had already gone over it in class. And when I say she went over it, she pretty much rewrote the book

~

on a chalk board. Dr. Dorai-Raj was her name, and chemistry was her game. I don't know how old she was, but she was a silver haired woman that would make the smartest kids feel like they were born behind a shed. She walked to and from work every day, and every day she would look at you like you didn't belong. Most people didn't like Dr. Dorai-Raj, because she didn't seem helpful. She didn't seem very nice. But, when you talked to her, you learned about her past and her love for her husband.

SWEET STORY TIME!

One day that I remember so vividly was the day that I was walking to my Chemistry lab. As I walked across the campus, I came across a group of people kicking and screaming at a dog. It was a medium sized dog that probably was about a year or two old. One person grabbed the dog by the tail and started swinging it. Anyone of my friends would tell you, I don't like it when people mistreat animals. I ran over there, swinging my back pack at those fools! I hit one of them, while using some obscene language, and had them running away from the poor dog. When I got done with those idiots, I went back to the dog and made sure he was ok. The dog turned out to be super friendly, and now I was in a predicament. It was warm outside, and I had to go inside. I couldn't take the dog into my dorm, nor could I leave the dog in my car during a 2 plus hour lab period. I had to go to lab because I had not fully grasped the concept of chemistry. So, I picked up the dog and went to class. As soon as I got there, I went straight for Dr. Dorai-Raj and pleaded my case: terrible people where outside, I had no leash, I couldn't take him to the dorm, and I couldn't leave him in my car. If she would allow me to keep the dog in the lab for the duration, as soon as I finished, I would take the dog to the animal shelter. I was sure he would be adopted; he was one of the nicest dogs I had ever met. Dr. Dorai-Raj reluctantly agreed, and I put the dog down near the door and went to my station to do my lab. I rushed through the work so that the dog wouldn't be in there longer than necessary. As I finished up and got ready to go, Dr. Dorai-Raj stopped me. She said "I'll take him." To my surprise, she had fallen for the cute face during the time that I was working. I hadn't even paid attention to the fact that he had already nestled up to her feet and had fallen for her too. For the rest of my time at Stillman, whenever I would see Dr. Dorai-Raj walking home from Stillman, I would see a medium sized dog on a leash walking with her.

Chapter 2

PUT THEM INTO PROGRAMS
THAT WILL HELP THEM SUCCEED

When I was in elementary school – probably around the third grade, I took a test outside of school, and they put me into the GATE program. GATE stands for Gifted And Talented Education. At the time, I didn't really know what that meant, but I found out soon enough. What it meant to me was that I no longer had summers off. During the summer, I went to GATE programs where I had to do extra math and reading assignments. I don't know if you read that right, but my summers consisted of MORE CLASSES! At that young age, I wasn't fully aware that every summer, students were afforded a full summer to run around with friends, be lazy, wake up late, and generally do nothing but eat and watch television. I thought all students continued studies throughout the summer, so I didn't complain. I had to wake up early and go to these classes, I had homework that I had to turn in, and everyone was so serious about it that I didn't really make friends. I was there for one purpose, and one purpose only…. to do additional school work. I didn't hate it, but I didn't love it either.

When I was in the fifth grade at Maxwell Park Elementary, I was chosen, along with one other pupil from my class, to attend a summer enrichment program at one of the most prestigious private schools in Oakland, Head Royce. It was so prestigious that I didn't even know it existed. If you can't afford the school, then you don't even mention the school's name. The summer after fifth grade, I was driven up there to find one of the largest school campuses I had ever seen. It was broken up into three levels. The elementary school was on the bottom, and it had its own play area, library, and cafeteria. The next level was the pool. Right above that was the junior high school level, with their own library (which was just as large as the public library that I had gone to find books) and cafeteria. Then, there was the high school. Right above the high school was the basketball gym, the baseball diamond, and an open field that I think was for soccer, football, or whatever sport that needed open space.

After I got over the amazement of the campus, I was back to doing what I already did every summer, take more classes and learn more stuff. I started French lessons on top of swimming, English, and science. I basically went to year around schools every day and had very little breaks. Yet, I had fun! I made new friends from other elementary schools, I learned new things, and I finally was able to learn how to swim, even though in the Oakland hills in the summer time is cold as hell in the mornings. I had an amazing time going to the library, going into the expansive cafeteria, and playing on the open field. We were definitely not the only students there. Head Royce had summer school every summer for gifted students, their own in which the parents had to pay, and the rest of us that was there on scholarship. But, we intermingled with everyone and no one felt left out. I went to the summer program for two years before transitioning into a summer school junior counselor. I was a counselor for two years, and since we were older kids and we got to tell the younger kids what to do. Since I loved science and animals, I worked in the lower school with the elementary kids in the science classroom. It was my job to feed and take care of the many animals that lived in the classroom. There was a large python and two smaller snakes, birds, rats, mice, guinea pig, and hissing cockroaches (ew!!!!!). Sometimes the teacher would bring in her two golden retrievers.

Every morning, we still had classes to take, but for the afternoons, we worked in our various counselor duties. My favorite thing was to take the python out, put him around my shoulders, and walk around the campus scaring people. They could not fathom how I was not scared of the snake, nor why it wasn't deciding to choke me, although one day he tried. I had to unwrap him and put him back in the cage that day. Takes me to another memory, when I was in the 5-6 grades, my best friend and I would walk around the edge of our school yard and collect pill bugs. We would make little habitats for them and everything. But, our favorite time was after it rained. Since there was a lot of dirt and bushes around the gates, we would collect pill bugs, worms, and snails as they seeked shelter. We would pick them and chase our classmates all around the school – boys and girls. To say we were tom boys is probably an understatement.

After the Head Royce program was over, I was well into junior high. I attended Montera Junior High, and was coming into my own. I was also realizing that most students didn't go to summer programs like I did, and I wanted to stop going all together, but my mother really wasn't having it. I think I had one summer off, but the summer after my ninth grade year, my best friend and I went off to Space Camp. First, we went to Arkansas, and my mother showed us her alma mater, University of Arkansas Pine Bluff. She tried to get us interested in the school, but we were not, so I don't remember much of what happened. Then, we got into a rental car and drove to Louisiana to Southern University, where my older brother and sister studied. Although we thought we were grown and tried to hang out with them, we were not allowed to and spent most of the time walking around the campus learning only that we wish we were grown.

Flashback – one night at my brother's apartment, my best friend and I was laying on our bed (the floor) talking. We started playing around, and I hit her in the head with a pillow. She never forgot. It took her almost a year to hit my back, and when she did, she reminded me of that night. That was when I realized that my friend is a bucket holder, and will always remember what someone did to her so that she could get them back.

After visiting campuses, we got down to Huntsville, AL where Space Camp was to commence. At the camp, we learned all about space travel, how it worked, and what happens to you in space. I took even more classes, but they were intertwined with videos and field trips. It was during this time that I went into my very first IMAX theater, when these theaters were only for museums and things like that, and not in every major city in America. We watched a video on space travel that was so amazing, that for a split second, I thought this could be something that I wanted to do when I grew up. Mostly what I remember though about Space Camp was that the food was HORRIBLE! My best friend and I mostly ate salads because there was a salad bar, and the only way to mess that up was to mess up your own salad. Secondly, I remember them giving us space suits to wear around, which was cool. Another thing I remember was getting into a large tank and scuba diving. Putting on all the gear, learning that your eyes and ears will mess up if you come up to fast, and diving all the way down was so amazing! When we got to the bottom of the tank, there was a large metal ball that they said weighed about a ton. But down there, it was easy to lift and easy to throw to my friend (thanks to physics!). We had so much fun in the tank that I didn't want to leave. Lastly, I remember there was a student from South America that had a thick accent. There were also two guys from Oakland too, yet they acted like they were so hard and that no one could beat them. They were annoying. Well, one day we were walking in a wooded area, and the South American guy picks up a pine cone and tosses it high in the air above the two guys from Oakland. I think it hit one of them in the head and they turned around ready to fight. The South American looks up and says "those trees, those F****** trees!" This seemed to satisfy them, because they looked up and got mad at the trees! Hilariousness!

Programs In Your Area For Your Child(ren)

_____

_____

_____

_____

_____

_____

_____

_____

_____

_____

_____

_____

_____

_____

_____

_____

_____

_____

_____

_____

_____

_____

_____

_____

_____

_____

_____

The next summer, I swam for a summer swim team that by best friend was a part of. I had only learned to swim a few summers before and really didn't have any practice, so I was not the best swimmer. In fact, I don't believe I ever won a race. I definitely didn't help with the relay races and when I did the back stroke for my team, I ALWAYS ran into the lines in the pool. It was sad, but I had fun. And that was yet another summer that I didn't have free. The following summer, I worked at McDonald's.

My junior year, I took Marine Biology, and I LOVED that class. Encinal is situated in Alameda, California, where behind the buildings is the football field and the baseball field, and behind that is an estuary. In that class, we learned all about the marine creatures that lived in our estuary and in the bay as well as the ocean. As a part of the class, we all had to put on hip waders and walk into the estuary to collect samples. Yes, some people got their boots stuck and fell in, which meant large amounts of water went into the waders and stayed there, lucky I was not one of those people. We collected plants, bivalves, and many other things and took them back to class, where there was a 50-gallon tank. With the teacher's assistance, we set up the tank with all of our collections, and studied how they moved and ate right there in class. It was in that class that I learned about the brackish water in our backyard – water that is half fresh water and half salt water. It was amazing. My teacher saw how I took to the class and sent me home with information for my parents about ANOTHER summer program. This program was called NYLF – National Youth Leadership Forum. Since I was interested in science, the one I was given was on medicine. In that program, you were able to go to an appointed school for the summer and learn what it is like to go to med school. The following summer, I went to UCLA and learned about med school and what it took to go there. At the time, I thought I may want to be an OB/GYN. I took the classes, learned a lot, and was able to have some time away from family for a while, which was cool. After you finish a summer program with NYLF-MED, they invite you to travel outside of the country with them to learn about medicine in other countries. The following summer, I was able to go to China, and three years later, I went to Australia. It was utterly amazing.

Chapter 3

IT STARTS EARLY
AND IT STARTS WITH YOU

I was speaking to some college-aged students about education in school, and the group that I was talking to said they never liked science or math. I asked them why not, and their reason was simple – their parents weren't interested in it, so they in turn where not interested in it. As we dived deeper into this reason, they explained that, while growing up they loved to read. Two spoke of fond memories of their mother reading to them every night. Since she read to them as children, they grew up loving to read. We talked about the different books that they read, which included Goosebumps, but also Harry Potter series and books on things like Pokémon and other fictious cartoons. But the main point is that their mother read to them. She introduced them to words on a page that took you to a wondrous land of make believe. Because of that early introduction, they chose to continue down that path, reading things that interested them. Unfortunately, those books were not science or math related. Their mother didn't have the interested to seek out books that talked about science and math, and when they were old enough to go to school, they didn't have an introduction to those things. For all of the students that I talked to, their parents didn't have a real interest in math and science, and when they needed help with their homework, the parents couldn't – or didn't help them because they either didn't understand it or they didn't have an interest in it themselves.

Here in lies the problem. I am not saying that all parents must have an interest in all things, but you do have to have an understanding, or at least the desire to learn it so that you can help your children succeed. When a child comes home with homework that you don't understand, we live in a technology based society, where you both can go to the computer and Google the answer. You have to bring a desire of knowledge and understanding to course work so that the children can see that and want to do it as well. Kids eventually grow up and will have their own interests and desires, but when they are young and starting elementary school, they are still sponges that will like what their parents like, or like what is introduced to them time and time again. It can be hard or daunting to find books or materials on a variety of subjects, but it helps in the long run to introduce kids to different things so that they can choose from it themselves as they get older. One thing that the college students told me was they wished it was different and their parents that had interests in science, math, history, business, or politics. If they were introduced to it at an early age, maybe they would have had more interest and learned more about it, thus helping them as they got older.

Chapter 4

LEARN ABOUT THEIR DREAMS, THEN HELP THEM

You need to take time and talk to children. The younger you talk to them, the more open they are to having dreams. When you talk to a student in kindergarten or first grade, their minds are open and they believe that they can be anything, including superman or superwoman. As that child gets older, they begin to marginalize themselves. Nature and nurture starts to play a role in what children think they can become. Grades place them into categories of who is smart and who is not. They start to see their passions dwindle if they lack encouragement, and that is where you step in. LISTEN to them. Not only listen to what they say, but how they say it, and how it makes them feel. When you sit down with kids of any age, they have slight inflections in their voices when they talk about what they love to do verses what they like to do. Their eyes get bigger and brighter when they talk about their love verses what they like. And, when they say what they love, encourage them even if you don't know what it is or how they will achieve it.

Let me give you an example: suppose you have a son that says he loves superman, and wants to be superman when he grows up. How would you encourage him to become superman in his own right? First, you must ask him why he wants to be superman in the first place. What is it about superman that he likes and why does he want to be like him? Now, if your son answers that he loves superman because he helps people, then your son may be the type of person that wants to serve and protect. There are many ways that he can do that. He can do it in the armed forces, as a policeman, fireman, or even a paramedic. But, the list doesn't stop there – he may want to work the nonprofit aspect or even as a doctor with Doctors Without Borders. There are many things that your son can do that deals with helping others and making sure people are safe and taken care of. Now, let's say your son loves superman because superman can fly. Well, even with the way technology is advancing every day, we have not come up with a way to make one-man fly with superpowers, but we do fly. Your son may want to be a pilot, or work in aviation. Just because your son has a fictional character that he looks up to, there are real attributes to each one. If you spend the time talking with your child to see what it is that they like and why they like it, then you have an opportunity to find something in them that drives them. You will discover their passion if you will. You find the passion, or dream, and you nurture and encourage it.

What if the dream that your child has is something you know nothing about, then what? Don't stop encouraging because you don't understand, instead find someone that understands it and can encourage that child for you. Yet, never give your child to a mentor without knowing the fundamentals. Learn what you can about the profession so that you can talk to them about it in an intellectual way. One thing that all kids need is someone to talk to about their love, and if you are a parent, guardian, or someone in this child's life consistently, then you are probably the person that they want to talk to about their day. If you have a working understanding, then you can spend more time with them discussing that particular field and getting them engaged in other ways. You can also ask questions, and most of the time, they will want to share what they know and how they learned about it. Another thing is, the more they talk about it and the more they practice it, the more they will understand it themselves. The one way to master something is to teach it, and the more you teach it and talk about it, the more it becomes ingrained in your mind.

What Does Your Child Like To Do? Who Do They Look Up To?

_____

_____

_____

_____

_____

_____

_____

_____

_____

_____

_____

_____

_____

_____

_____

_____

_____

_____

_____

_____

_____

_____

_____

_____

Let me give you an example: Let's say you work in business and you can teach your child all the ends and outs of working in a business, how to balance the books, and how to talk to people in the field, but your child wants to be an engineer – something you know nothing about. Well, one thing you will want to teach your child is networking, but we will discuss that in another chapter. Use your resources, Google it, or ask your child's teacher for programs and mentorships in engineering. Don't stop there! Learn about the field as best you can so that you can be a helpful guide into engineering. The list of specialties in engineering can be daunting, you have electrical, mechanical, structural, bio, and many more engineering specialties, so you want to talk to your child and learn what it is about engineering that they love. When you know something about the field, they can come talk to you freely about their likes and dislikes. They can talk to you about their fears and dreams, and you can be the one that helps guide them as they progress through school and on to college. Once they get to a point when they graduate and actually begin working, you should have enough knowledge of the field to have long conversations about it and what they like to do.

Now, you may be thinking that you don't have time, energy, or even a desire to learn a new subject for the sake of your child. If you are this type of person, take a step back and ask what you planned to do when your child found their dream? Their dreams may not line up with yours and then what? Did you plan to just stop talking to them about it and only discuss things like sports, weather, news, or fashion? There is nothing wrong with those examples and if that is what you talk about, then good. But – think about yourself and how it was when you were growing up. Did you ever have dreams or passions, music or clothes interests, or even interests in boys or girls that didn't line up with your parents, and therefore you could never talk to them about it? How did it make you feel? Did you want to have a more open dialogue with them about the work you do, or did you ever want them to just UNDERSTAND the work that you do/did? If it is rocky for you to talk to your parents about your dreams, do you want that same feeling to be between you and your child? I hope the answer is no and you take it into account when your son comes to you and says he wants to be superman when he grows up.

As your child gets older, their dreams may change. If you are there with them from the beginning, talking to them about their dreams, you should be able to see how they change and when they start to change. This usually happens towards the end of elementary school and beginning of middle school. It is during this time that children start to identify themselves through groups and cliques. It is during this time as well when they have been subjected to copious amounts of media influence through television, billboards, movies, video games, digital media, and social media. It is also during this time when you should monitor what they are watching and what is influencing them as they migrate through portrays of men and women. Sometimes, their dreams don't seem to match reality but it is important not to squash the dreams, but explain to them the reality. For example, your daughter may love Serena Williams and want to play tennis like her, but only one problem – she is 13 and just picked up a tennis racket two weeks ago, and it has been sitting in the same spot for the last week. Now, it is important not to discourage her and tell she can't do it, because she could do it – if she starts practicing ASAP! Explain to her that Serena didn't get to her level of expertise overnight. She practices… A LOT! So, when her friends want to go to the movies or out to the mall, she may have to skip that time for tennis practice. She may have to forgo summer just hanging with friends to attend tennis camp and practice in the mornings before school starts. If she can do that, then she may have a chance to be as good as Serena Williams, or even better than her, but it takes practice and determination. If she cannot give up hanging with friends during the summer for this, then maybe she can shift her dreams a bit. She can still take tennis practice, but what else does she like? Maybe she is good at math? One way she can get the tennis lessons for free or cheap is by tutoring the tennis teacher's child in math for exchange for lessons. This will help her get her skills up in math while getting her skills up in tennis. A win win!

Encouragement doesn't stop when they graduate from high school. It is important to continue encouraging them when they go to college. College for a lot of students is a wakeup call. In college, oftentimes students can readily identify what they have and have not learned based upon how well they can keep up with and understand the coursework. They don't have their parents waking them up for school or making them breakfast. They are on their own to get up, go to class, and do their homework. If they feel like they are failing and want to quit, encourage them to continue. Let them know that you are there for them and will help support their dreams in any way that you can.

What Are Your Goals For Helping Your Child?

_____

_____

_____

_____

_____

_____

_____

_____

_____

_____

_____

_____

_____

_____

_____

_____

_____

_____

_____

_____

_____

_____

_____

_____

Chapter 5

MENTORS ARE IMPORTANT

Mentors are very important for kids, and for adults. This next chapter can be incorporated into your life as well. When it comes to doing what you want to do, it is important to find someone that is already doing it, and ask for their help. Nine times out of ten, they are willing to help you because they too had someone who helped them along the way. But, this is not the case for everyone. Some people will flat out say no, and sometimes, you won't even make it to the hello before you realize that that person does not want to be bothered by you. If you run into these types of people, that is ok. Maybe they weren't supposed to be you or your child's mentor, and you should move on. If no one else is doing what you want to do, and this person is the Oprah of your desired career, then keep asking for the help. Ask others along the way and grab onto as many mentors as you can. Yet continue asking for the individual you really want to mentor you.

Do not find one person for your child to be mentored by, but multiple. If your child loves biology, loves animals, and loves the violin, then it would be helpful to find people in all of those fields. I am sure you can find a veterinarian in your area that can mentor your child, but you may have trouble with the violin and biology part. That is where schools can be helpful. See if you can find someone at a local college that teaches biology or is a biologist themselves. They can talk to you and your child all about the work that they do and also give you contacts to the people they know doing all kinds of work. This may help your child in the future. Maybe being a vet is not for them, but zoology is. By talking out the requirements and job duties for each career, your child will have a better understanding of how to navigate through college without changing their major multiple times. Maybe your child learns that being a local vet is not for them, but being a vet at a zoo or another animal enclosure fits them best. Again, by talking it out with professionals, it will help guide them in what to take in college and what to major in.

When I was growing up, I didn't have any real mentors. I wanted to work with animals and become a vet, but I didn't know any vets personally, so I was never able to question them about their work. If I could go back in time, I would have begged my parents to help me find a veterinarian that would have let me volunteer at their hospital and learn more about what they did. I did, however volunteer at our local animal shelter and learned what the technician (not vet) did there, which was administer meds and euthanize animals. Nothing more.

I didn't get my first mentor until I went to college. At Stillman College, I had the pleasure of working with some phenomenal professors. I drew closest to Dr. Aggison, Dr. Washington, and Dr. Krotzer. These three where my biological sciences' professors and I admired them. There was only one problem: they were NOT veterinarians. They did help me a lot with my biological sciences, and even helped me get internships in herpetology and neurobiology, and I learned what it took to work in a lab. Unfortunately, I did not want to work in a lab. That was never the dream. The dream was to work as a veterinarian, and in the small town of Tuscaloosa, Alabama, I never met a veterinarian that would allow me into their hospital to learn about what they did.

Despite the fact that my mentors where not in the field in which I wanted to eventually go, I still learned a lot from them. One thing that sticks out that one of my mentors claimed he did was is if he was in his office, but did not feel like speaking to any students, he would just close the door. When a student came by knocking, just whisper 'come in.' When that student walked away and came back later asking where he was, he would tell them I was in the office and said come in, you just didn't hear me!

Seriously though, they looked out for my fellow biology students and I. They tutored us when we were unsure of the materials, they lectured us when they knew that we could do better, but didn't, and they made sure we stayed on track to graduate in a timely fashion. They continued to look out for you well after you graduate. About two years after I graduated from Stillman College, I received an email from Dr. Aggison and Dr. Washington – both of them had moved on to University of Connecticut, and where in charge of diversifying their PhD program. They wanted to know if I would apply to the school and move there to receive my PhD! I applied, was accepted, and moved up there within three months! Although I was there for the summer and one semester, I realized that I did NOT like the program, because it was not my dream. I should have known that, and perhaps my mentors should have known that, but what they wanted to instill in me was that if I just got a PhD in anything, including microbiology, I could go on to do whatever I wanted as a scientist. But, I could not see myself going through 5-6 years of a combined Masters and PhD program in microbiology. It's not that I couldn't do it, but rather I had no real desire to do it.

After realizing this, I left Connecticut and moved back to Dallas, TX, where I was initially after graduating from Stillman. While there, I went to work as a vet tech and learned firsthand what veterinarians did. I also learned that I was not interested in that work at all! After working for a few years as a vet tech, I realized one thing – it is rarely about what you know but who you know. Although I had been at one of my jobs for a year or less, I saw many people that should not have been given promotions receive promotions because they were either friends or family members of the person promoting them. Do not get me wrong, I have no ill will towards any of the people in these scenarios, in fact I still call some of them my friends, but what I do know is that someone who is educated, has experience, and has worked in a managerial position before should be given a chance for a promotion over someone who only has a little experience and is friends or family of the person doing the promoting. Here is an example of when I really realized that it was all about who you know: I worked at a vet hospital in Dallas, TX that was broken up into three parts. There was the reception area, the middle area where medicines where located and you had access to the patient/client rooms, and then the back surgical area where procedures where done. With three rooms, there were three managers over them. The person over the reception area was married to the person over the middle room, and the person over the middle room was the cousin to the person over the surgical area. Everyone was related! Also, there were another cousin/sister of those three that worked there as well. As well as a mother/son team. They looked out for one another and if you came in like I did with no family or friends working there, even with more education and experience, you didn't get any promotions at the job, in fact you weren't even considered!

So, I left that job, decided to go back to school, and work on my networking skills. Networking is very important for it is what helps you get the job when you share the same amount of qualifications and experience as other people vying for the same job.

List Some Possible Mentors For Your Child

_____

_____

_____

_____

_____

_____

_____

_____

_____

_____

_____

_____

_____

_____

_____

_____

_____

_____

_____

_____

_____

_____

_____

_____

Chapter 6

NETWORK

Networking is very important. When you go out somewhere, it is important to find out what people do and also tell them what you are doing and what you want to do. You never know who you are going to meet and how they may affect your life or how you may affect theirs. Networking starts with one thing – saying hello. If you have a child, it is important to start teaching them how to network when they get to the fourth or fifth grade. It is during this time that they are more inclined to remember people, know what they may want to do with their lives, and be mindful of their surroundings and situations. You can start at your job with teaching them how to be confident and how to network.

First things first, put away the smartphone or tablet! Right now, one way to pacify kids is to give them something to look at while you do something else. This usually comes in the form of a smartphone or tablet where they can play games, watch videos, or chat with friends. How will they ever meet anyone if they are constantly looking down at a screen.

One thing you can do is take your child to work and have them introduce themselves to your coworkers and bosses. When you introduce your child to someone at work, introduce them like you would introduce a friend or companion. You can say, "Bob, I would like you to meet Steve. Bob, Steve is my co-worker here at [blank] company, and Steve, Bob is my son." Teach your child to raise his or her hand in order to shake the hand of your coworker and shake hands firmly! Even if you think it is unlady like to give a firm handshake, when it comes to business and meeting people that may help you in the long run, it is better to give a firm handshake than a limp one - do not expect them to kiss the top of your hand or give you a curtsey, that is not how it works in the business world.

Once they have met your coworker, your child should be comfortable in asking what they do. And I do mean ASK, not demand. Your child should not say, "So, what do you do?" That is impolite and demanding, and most people would not like being spoken to like that. Instead, they should ask politely, "May I ask, what do you do?" When asking in this polite manner, it makes the other person comfortable and even impressed by the demeanor of your child. They can explain what they do and if it is something that is interesting to your child, they can ask for more information. How they got there? What school they went to? What did they study? All of these follow up questions will serve your child in the future when they meet other people and are trying to determine if it is something that can be beneficial in the future. Even if it is not something that you see as beneficial, ask for a business card anyway and to offer them yours (if you have one as a parent). The reason for this is because if someone is impressed by you, and realize they know someone that can help you, or vise versa, there is a way to contact each other.

Teach them that one way for people to help you is for them to see you helping others. Everything is circular and what you do for others reflects on the person that you are and in turn, others will help you. Also, teach your child to talk about their dreams and desires. People that they meet may not be able to help, but they may know people who can. Never disregard anyone or catch an attitude with anyone. You never know who they know and how they may be able to help you.

Ways You Can Help Your Child Network

For me, it started with the idea that I wanted to film women in STEM for my Master's thesis. One of the places that I wanted to film was at Chabot Space and Science Center, a great place for astronomy and space science related adventures! I tried cold emailing them, but I only found the info email and I received no response when I emailed them. So, I pretty much gave up finding anyone there to film, and was ok with that. One day, I was walking my dog in my neighborhood and ran into a classmate from middle school. We hadn't seen each other since middle school, but we recognized each other right away! So, I stopped and we chatted for a while catching up with one another. He told me that he was a firefighter now, and I told him about the project I was working on. Turned out, he knew someone at Chabot from an event that they shared, and promptly called her while I was standing there! She in turn said she was busy, but told him to give me her email and phone number. I emailed her as soon as I got home. I had no idea that my middle school classmate that did NOT work in my field would be my ticket into a science center I had previously emailed with no response.

Well, within a day, the woman I emailed gave me the number to the person over media relations – a woman named Autumn. After a few emails with Autumn, it was set up that I would come and interview four amazing women that worked in Astronomy, Chemistry, and Education. So, my videographer and I went up the Chabot and met with all the ladies. While there, I told Autumn how much I admired Bill Nye and Neil DeGrasse Tyson, and how I would love to meet them. Well, Autumn tells me I just missed Dr. Tyson for he had been there recently (cue the tears), and asked me if I wanted to see pictures of her and Dr. Tyson. I of course said "Hecks no! I don't want to see pictures of you with my idol! Crazy!" We laughed and I finished all the interviews. Unfortunately, (or fortunately) I missed saying bye to Autumn when we left and wasn't able to say thank you, so I emailed her. And you know what she did? She sent me an email with pictures of her and Dr. Tyson! So, I responded that I was upset to see the pictures of her and Dr. Tyson, but if Bill Nye was coming any time soon, please tell me so that I can meet him. She discreetly called me and told me that Bill Nye was coming to do a talk in a two weeks and the registration was closed, but she would put my name on the list if I wanted to go! Um, heck yes I wanted to go!

I showed up to the event beaming! I had an opportunity to see Bill Nye up close and personal. Although I wasn't supposed to be there, I managed to get a seat in the second row. Bill Nye gave an excellent talk on climate change that included a story about his parents while growing up. At the end of the talk, he asked the audience if there were any questions. My hand shot up so quickly that he nodded for me to be the first question. I asked him as plainly as I could (although I am sure I had a kool aid wide smile on my face) "When will there be a science program on television with a woman host?" Bill Nye responded with a story about his mother: while he was young, his mother had called a service to order an America Express card. The operator told her that she was married, and that her husband could order a card, but she could not have one in her own name. With this story, Bill Nye talks about how times have changed since he was young, and that anyone can have an American Express card now. So, times are still changing, and that a female science host was due, and that I could be that person.

I thought so too!

Chapter 7

SUMMERS ARE FOR LEARNING TOO

*D*o not just give your child full summers off to watch tv, play video games, or sit around. If you cannot afford a full summer program, that is ok. At least try to occupy some of their summer with a program that suits them and gets them active or thinking. It is ok to have homework in the summer. I did and I turned out fine (somewhat). If you feel bad – don't. In the future, they will thank you for giving them a structured summer when they were young. It gets harder to do this as the child becomes a teenager and starts making lifelong friendships, but do not give up. One thing that you can do is meet the parents of your child's friends and encourage them to put their child in the same programs that your child is in so that your child doesn't feel alone. If the state that you live in is as awesome as my state, California, there should be some state or even city sponsored programs that are free or low cost that you can enroll your child in during the summer. If you can afford it, and you are comfortable with them at a certain age, send them off to camp. They will find out that they can survive, make friends, and even have fun. It will teach them responsibility with their actions and their time, and it gives you time to yourself.

List Summer Programs In Your Area

_____

_____

_____

_____

_____

_____

_____

_____

_____

_____

_____

_____

_____

_____

_____

_____

_____

_____

_____

_____

_____

_____

_____

_____

_____

Chapter 8
THEY
NEED A JOB

As your child gets to working age, typically 15 or 16, encourage them to get a summer job. If they are going to apply for the job, make sure they know how to be respectful and conscientious of how they look. If you are a hiring manager, would you hire a student with green hair? Or one that has sagging pants down below their butts? Most, if not all professionals would not. SO, even if your child is a trendsetter or follows trends, make sure they do not take that trend to their first interview. Even if the job is flipping burgers, they need to learn early on that what makes you stand out from the rest is your first appearance, and no professional will hire someone with pink hair, or skinny jeans that hang off their ass. Now, I am not trying to take away from a student's personality or style, but I am offering you advice for going into the real world as a professional. If you are handling large sums of money and have to make a deal with an overseas investor, they probably would not like, or could even be offended by facial jewelry, clothes that look unkempt, or unnatural colored hair. You may be saying 'oh they are a teenager and that is what teenagers do,' but teaching them early to be mindful of how they look and act at their job. Unless they are an entrepreneur in a field that doesn't mind it. Because, even as an entrepreneur, if your business gets big and draws attention from the big players, they may not deal with you because of how you act. The truth hurts sometimes.

Where Do You Want Your Child To Work?
Where Do They Want To Work?

_____

_____

_____

_____

_____

_____

_____

_____

_____

_____

_____

_____

_____

_____

_____

_____

_____

_____

_____

_____

_____

Chapter 9

TRAVEL

If you have the means, take your children out of their environment. Another way to state that – travel! Take your child away from home to a place they may not even know exists. This helps especially when a child complains a lot about what they don't have. If they complain about what they don't have, take to a place where there is even less. Road trips can save you money and draw your family close. You can go in your car, rent a car or van, or even rent a motor home. If you have a family that you spend time with, you can rent the motor home with them, save on the cost, and travel to motor home parks. They are more fun than you think and can give your child a different perspective of what is around them.

When I was a child, my family had an orange van. This was in the 80s, and the van's seats in the back folded out into a bed. They were side seats that looked like benches in the back, and there were a few cabinets that you could store snacks in for the trip. During that time, we would travel from Oakland, CA down to through to Arkansas. This was WELL before tablets, DVD players, or any other electronic that will keep your child quiet. We listened to the radio until the radio went out, and we didn't have satellite radio to find tunes. If someone was diligent enough, they could sit up front and try to find a radio station that played the music we liked, but 9 times out of 10, when you are in the middle of no man's land, there is no radio station playing anything. We relied on books, card games, or (gasp) talking to one another for entertainment.

SIDE NOTE: it is time to take the electronics out of your kids hands and put a book in it. Encourage them to read instead of playing all the time. Even if the book is about the video game itself, it will help their reading skills.

Road trips can be fun, entertaining, as well as knowledge builders. You can find books or apps on where you are going and what you are passing along the way. Interesting topics can be things like geography, botany, biology, ecology, or even technology. Notice those windmills on the hill as you drive by? How do they work? Are they good for the environment, bad for the environment, or both? This is a topic that you can bring up with your child as you drive, and make it into meaningful conversation. It also helps them with critical thinking skills and makes them think outside of the box. And that is what we want for the future right? Kids that learn about critical thinking and take it into adulthood.

When you take them places that they heard about or read about it class, it brings their lesson to life. When I was in junior high, my mother took me to Birmingham to visit the church where the four girls were killed by a bomb. We walked the now museum, read about it, and felt the tragedy that happened right there many years before I was born. She also took us the burial site of Dr. Martin Luther King Jr., the civil rights museum, and countless places that told of African-American history. When you see with your own eyes the places that had to deal with evil, it opens you up to wanting to learn more.

It is most important that the places you visit makes your child appreciate home all the more. My mother grew up in Magnolia, AR and she had an aunt that lived in Cullen, LA. We went to visit her aunt, and she lived in the middle of nowhere. Now, I grew up middle class. We had a TV in the living room that had all the channels and a TV in my parents' room as well as the kitchen that only got local channels. If someone, especially my father, was in the living room watching TV, you had to go watch your programs on one of the other TVs, which was okay because most programs that you wanted to watch came on the local channels anyway. Well, when we went to that particular aunt's house, in the south, in the middle of summer, we had to deal with the fact that she had one television that only got local channels. Not only that, her house was a two bedroom, so that mean we had to double and triple up on beds in the middle of the heat of the summer in Louisiana – with no air conditioning. If you have gone your entire life not experiencing a summer in the south, you are lucky. Most places have air conditioning, but some places in the middle of nowhere like my aunt's house, do not. So, you are laying on a bed with another human and their hot skin and breath, on sheets that you both are sweating on, and you can't breathe. The first night we were there was terrible! It got worse in the morning. That morning, I was one of the first to get up, probably because I barely got any sleep anyway, and I went into the dark kitchen. I turned on the lights, and dozens of small dark creatures ran for cover. There were roaches everywhere! Needless to say, I screamed, barely ate breakfast, and probably lost some weight that summer. I never was the first one up and in the kitchen again, and eventually I learned to respect the show Passions, because that was what my aunt watched every day. I got to go outside and learned to respect what I had at home. I didn't ask why I didn't have this or that because I knew I that I had it better than some of the kids that lived in Cullen, where my aunt lived.

Name Some Places You Can Visit By Driving

_____

_____

_____

_____

_____

_____

_____

_____

_____

_____

_____

_____

_____

_____

_____

_____

_____

_____

_____

_____

_____

_____

_____

If you can, take them out to the country, or put them in a program that allows them to go out of the country. When I was in high school, I was placed in a program called NYLF – National Youth Leadership Forum, and the one that I picked was medicine. When I was 18, I traveled with a group to China. It was one of the most amazing experiences of my life. Although we stayed in hotels and ate mostly at restaurants, we were also taken to villages to see how some people lived in different provenances. The point of the trip was to compare Western Medicine to Eastern Medicine. We visited hospitals and medical schools and saw firsthand how they operated. We also went to villages and met medicine men and acupuncturist. One of my experiences that made me realize how good we have it in Oakland was when we were in a remote village and I had to go to the bathroom. I am taller than the average woman, but by no means am I really tall at 5'7", but I am taller than most people in China. The 'bathroom' was a clay and brick three-walled building that didn't have a toilet, just a hole in the ground. It was a bathroom for the whole village, and did not smell very well. I tried to brave the bathroom, but when I walked in, I realized that I had to bend way down, feel my way through the walls, and hover over a hole in the ground that I could not see…. and I had no tissue. I decided to hold it until we got back to the hotel, and I almost didn't make it. I sat in front of the bus, talked to no one, and jumped off as soon as the driver put the bus in park. I didn't listen to the leaders, and pushed my way in the hotel lobby while running for a bathroom!

That was just one memory that made me realize that Oakland was not half bad. Another thing that I experienced that made me feel better was the fact that we visited a market right outside of one of the medical schools. As I walked the market, I realized that it was summer, it was hot, and there were eggs everywhere! No refrigeration was in site, and some of the eggs had been buried for an extended amount of time and was considered a delicacy. There were also animals there that were being killed on the spot for fresh foods. I was intrigued and disgusted at the same time. It was mesmerizing to see some of this stuff, but it made you realize something: most Americans would be disgusted and want to find a grocery store, but we are not as healthy as most people in China. They have fresh meats and vegetables and barely, if ever, eat anything canned. They also do not thrive on medicines like we do as we grow older. They use homemade concoctions that seem to do the trick. So, who are we to determine that what they are doing is wrong?

My trip to China was great! I got to see the Terracotta warriors, the Great Wall, the largest waterfall in China, and many many other amazing things that you can only find there. It makes you realize that what you see on television or online does not even compare to the reality of it. I walked up the Great Wall of China and walked from one pillar to the other, and was out of breath! Yet, warriors would run through it warning each other of impending danger, and the architecture of it is amazing. It is one of the few manmade things that astronauts can see from space and I walked it! I touched it! I saw it, and that beats seeing it on television any day.

Make A Wish-List For Somewhere To Visit Out Of The Country

~

Chapter 10

INTRODUCE
THEM TO COLLEGE EARLY

*I*f possible, introduce them to college early. Most large cities have colleges, and even some of the smaller cities have community colleges that you can visit. One thing you can do as a family is take a course together at the local community college or even online. It is simple now to open a computer and get registered. I would suggest taking a language class, which would give your child a boost in the future. Or something fun like dancing or acting. Either way, open up their minds to the idea of being on a college campus. If you have younger siblings or cousins that are in college during the time that your child is growing up, take a weekend if you can and go visit them. You don't have to leave the state to do this. You can also just go to the campus yourself, or call and set up an appointment with a counselor to tour the schools, laboratories, stages, and/or dorm rooms. I suggest starting this towards the end of elementary through junior high. Place in their minds early that college is there and is a possibility for them to achieve. When they are in high school, if they have time, they can take a course at the local community college.

When I was in high school, my sister that is three years older than me, was not doing well in her biology class. Since this was the major I envisioned myself going into anyway, when my mother asked me if I would take the class with her and help her out, I was excited to go. We went to Laney College, which is a community college in Oakland and took biology together. There, I learned that even at that level, you could be lost in the classroom. I know there were more than 100 people in the stadium like class and there was no way for the teacher to know us all by name. Although I am used to sitting in the front, my sister wanted to sit in the back. The classroom was situated with an overhead projector and the professor went through each image in biology with technical terms and identification markers. I thought it was awesome as I looked around and realized I was probably the youngest person there. I took notes along with everyone else and bought scantrons to take the tests. I got an A out of the class and was actually happy to have taken the class.

Now, I know that not everyone is like me and may not enjoy taking biology when they are 15/16. So, I don't encourage taking it unless your child or student is interested in biological sciences anyway. There are many classes that they can take that can be transferred to their college or university once they graduate high school. From Arts to Astronomy or Economics to Theater, whatever your child or student is interested in, there is a program they can start as early as high school. And let's not forget online classes. There are extension programs at University of Berkeley and Harvard that you can take at your own pace and earn a grade. A lot of these programs will allow you to transfer the grade. Not all of the classes online can be transferred, but are good to know. For example, I know there are a lot of computer learning programs that you can take throughout a year and you can earn a certificate in coding. I know there are a lot of boot camps geared towards teaching coding. You can take them online or in class, all you have to do is Google it and find the nearest one in your area.

When I was in high school, I had two siblings in college – and they both went to Southern University. My mother made sure that while they were there, we went to visit them and see how it was to go to college. What I learned then, and from the college visitation trips , was that most HBCUs (Historically Black Colleges and Universities) are in the middle of nowhere! There may be a good reason for this: if you get rid of the temptation of fun, then the students would have no choice but to do their work. This may also be true for the PWIs (Predominately White Institutions) that are located in the middle of nowhere (think University of California Santa Cruz or University of Connecticut). I would like to think this is the reason, but it probably isn't. Either way, I thought it was interesting to see different dorms and how the students decorated their room to reflect who they were. I also learned about cafeteria food and often wondered how people gained "the freshman 15." That food was awful and there was nowhere to go to eat because the school was in the middle of nowhere! Thus, when I did go to college, one of the first things that my parents bought outside of toiletries was a small refrigerator and microwave. I ended up buying myself a toaster too because I was obsessed with bagels and English muffins, which are two things I barely eat today!

Make A List Of Colleges You Can Take Your Child To

_____

_____

_____

_____

_____

_____

_____

_____

_____

_____

_____

_____

_____

_____

_____

_____

_____

_____

_____

_____

_____

_____

_____

Chapter 11

THEY CAN'T BE WHAT
THEY CAN'T SEE

One thing that I am working on now is the fact that most students don't believe they can be what they can't see. What I mean by this is if there are no role models for them to look up to, then they may not be able to see themselves in that profession. Right now, most role models in the media are reality stars that are making a living being cruel or down right rude to their fellow cast mates.

Maybe that is my perception, but ask your 10 to 18-year-old child who their role model is. If it is someone who is in media and is either a male rapper or athlete, or a woman that is on a reality show or sings or raps while barely wearing any clothes, then there might be a problem. Next, why don't you ask them who their favorite scientist is? Who is their favorite techie, engineering, or math person? One of the problems with media is that they rarely show anyone in non-fictional STEM fields other than on PBS. Now, my outlook on reality television is my perception. I don't want anyone to think that I just hate these shows. Granted, I don't watch it, but it does give some people a glance into these people's lives as well as pay the participants. But, I cannot support them by watching the shows. What pains me is there are students in middle and high school that look up to reality stars, rappers, singers and athletes and will tell you that they want to be like them when they grow up. Now, I am not saying they shouldn't or couldn't do it, but why not have another suggestion for them?

The sad part is that there are great people in STEM doing wonderful things, that the mass media tries to hide behind fictional shows that only make a mockery of STEM professionals. Not all computer nerds have funky hairdos and plays with troll dolls or like to wear all black. Scientists are not all a bunch of nerdy guys and girls with no fashion sense and a weird obsession with sci-fi. There is a broad spectrum of people throughout STEM that you can introduce your child to, they just don't exist on television, but that is ok. There are remarkable people doing great things every day. I live in Oakland, which is a part of the Bay Area and very close to Silicon Valley. I virtually live in the world of startups and techie geniuses. Mix that in with University of California, Berkeley and University of California, San Francisco…there you have it! I am close to world renowned scientists and engineers. Financially, we are also home to the most non-profits in the nation, which means the money aka math, is in the building. If you live here, there is no shortage of STEM professionals that you can meet and introduce your child to.

If you don't live here, that is okay. You probably live close to colleges or even business that highlight Science, Technology, Engineering, or Math. You just have to know where to look. If you were to go online right now and type in one of these acronyms and your city, I can guarantee you that something will come up. In the event that I am wrong, or something pops up that does not interest your child, try reaching out to someone outside of your area. With the inventions of Skype, Facetime, Whatsapp, and all the other video platforms, you may be able to find someone that is in the field your child is interested in and get them to video chat with you and your child. The best thing about most people in these fields, is that they want to see students follow in their footsteps. With that being said, most of the time, they are more than happy to help and guide your child. Although these STEM professionals are willing to get involved and help your child, don't you fall by the wayside. It is important for you to be involved as well and keep abreast of the conversations and suggestions given by these professionals. They may encourage you to put your child into a program that will help them succeed. Research that program for yourself, and if there is a part for you as a parent to be involved, then by all means, BE INVOLVED! The more you know about the subject matter that your child is interested in, the better for the child.

List Professionals That You Would Like Your Child To Meet

_____

_____

_____

_____

_____

_____

_____

_____

_____

_____

_____

_____

_____

_____

_____

_____

_____

_____

_____

_____

_____

_____

_____

_____

~

Chapter 12

TEACHERS ARE IMPORTANT

Speaking of finding professionals and/or professors to help your student, it is important to start off with the teachers that they see every day. These are the professionals that help guide your child nine months out of the year. They also have to deal with your child nine months out of the year. You, as a parent should have a good rapport with ALL of your child's teachers from elementary to high school. I am not saying be a helicopter parent where you are always around your child, joining the PTA, bringing cupcakes every Friday, and knowing where your child's teacher lives! Please do not do that. Instead, just be an active parent that knows the teacher and have an expectation for your child to respect and honor their teachers as he/she goes through school. It is true, not every teacher is the best that they can be, and a lot of them have to deal with multiple students that may cause trouble, and some are just bad. This is why you as a parent should go to the parent's day and see what your child is doing. You can also meet the teacher in the beginning of the school year and know their expectations and goals for the incoming class. Help your child maintain those goals and opt for them to achieve the best that they can be. If the teacher is not a good teacher in your eyes, then perhaps you should switch your child out of that class.

I realize there is a fine line between being an active parent and a helicopter parent, but that may be a line you may have to walk, if you so choose. If your child is bringing home good grades and is noticeably learning, then the less you may have to do. If your child is not bringing home good grades and having trouble in school, then the more you may need to intercede. The basis of all of it is to help your child find their niche and pour into it. Whatever your child likes and decides to do, I can guarantee there is a STEM component to it.

If your student loves murals, then they must draw out their design on paper to map out how they want it to look on a wall. Basically, they are making a blue print for the design and have to take what they created on a smaller scale and make it larger. This is the same design thinking for an engineer as they plan a structure or building.

If your student is into finance, they will have to know math. They will have to know what it takes to generate a profit, i.e. counting money. If your student is interested in sports, then each time they practice, they are using physics to know where the ball is, where it needs to go, and how to get it there. So, for just about every profession, there is a significant amount of STEM within it. If your child is into video games, software, or apps, then they are into computer SCIENCE and technology. So, if your child says they are not into science, technology, engineering, or math, gently remind them that they are, they just haven't looked at it in the right way.

List Your Child's Teachers For The New School Year

_____

_____

_____

_____

_____

_____

_____

_____

_____

_____

_____

_____

_____

_____

_____

_____

_____

_____

_____

_____

_____

_____

_____

_____

_____

Chapter 13
HAVE EXPECTATIONS

You have to have expectations for your child's school performance. Unfortunately, we live in a time where every student is passed to the next grade, even if they do not do all their work. We also live in a time where a student is judged by their peers for the clothes they wear, the shoes they own, and the electronics that they have in their pockets. Oftentimes, intelligence is not held to as high esteem as outer wear. I have seen junior high school girls with long weaves and fake eyelashes, something that wasn't a big deal when I was in junior high. Apparently no one has told them that the glue from those fake eyelashes will pull out their real eyelashes to the point that they may not grow back. I have also seen junior high boys sagging skinny jeans, while wearing the newest Jordan's. Unfortunately, when you look at some of their grades, they are lacking severely.

Parents, I do not want to take away from your image or how you think your child should dress, nor do I want to take away from an individual expressing themselves with their style, but when that takes priority to a child's grades, then something is wrong. If your student is coming home with C's or below, then it will be extremely difficult for them to get into a college and nearly impossible for them to get grants or scholarships. This means financing their schooling will solely depend on you as a parent either right out of your pocket or through school loans. Also, if they are doing this bad in junior high or high school, what are the odds of them turning it around and graduating from college? These students must be aware that just because they will pass you in junior or high school, they will NOT just pass you through college. It is very possible to get kicked out for your grades and they will have no one to blame but themselves if they are not doing the work. If they get kicked out, someone (you or your child) still has to pay for the loans taken out. So, it is important to instill in them that maintaining good grades through junior high and high school will help them get scholarships and grants as well as get into college.

One suggestion that I have for parents if their students are not getting good grades is to take the money for the new Jordan's and get your child a tutor. Maybe take the money for the new iPhone and use it to place them in an after school program that helps them get their grades up. They will not be pleased by this and may cry or throw temper tantrums, but remind yourself that you are helping them reach higher heights in their future. They will thank you later. Besides, if they really feel the need to have the newest thing, help them find a job.

What Are Your Expectations For Your Child?

_____

_____

_____

_____

_____

_____

_____

_____

_____

_____

_____

_____

_____

_____

_____

_____

_____

_____

_____

_____

_____

_____

_____

Chapter 14

FIRST IMPRESSIONS
ARE IMPORTANT

I remember one time, many years ago, I stepped into a McDonalds to get some food. This was probably around 2010. While in there, I noticed a high school student in there for a job interview. This young lady was slouching in her seat, had a faux fur hooded puff coat on with the hood on her head, skinny jeans, and tennis shoes. Now, I have no idea if this young lady was hired or not, but I can tell you - in a professional setting, she definitely would not have been hired. I have also seen a young lady with green hair go to an interview at another fast food establishment, and a young man go to a local radio station with his pants sagging and a t-shirt on. And one time, on a train, I sat across from a young lady that was on the phone with a hiring manager and basically telling them that the reason she wanted the job was because she did, and they should just hire her. I cannot make this stuff up! These are all no no's, even for high school.

When I was in high school, I worked at a McDonalds in Oakland for the summer. When I went in for the interview, my parents made sure I had on clean khakis and a white shirt. I was not allowed to wear tennis shoes, but had to have on some nice black shoes. The reason why was because the hiring manager gets one opportunity to initially meet you and get a first impression. The hiring manager will take in how you dress, your make up, and your attitude. If your student has an attitude that the world owes them and they deserve the job, then they may take that attitude with them to college. That attitude does not work in the real world and it is something that they should learn from their very first job interview. It is your job as a parent to make sure they know that the world owes them nothing! They have to work harder than the multitude of people vying for the same job, the same grant, the same position. What makes them stand out in a positive way? This starts with the first job, and continues with them throughout their working career.

What Jobs Are Available For Your Child In Your Area?

_____

_____

_____

_____

_____

_____

_____

_____

_____

_____

_____

_____

_____

_____

_____

_____

_____

_____

_____

_____

_____

_____

_____

EPILOGUE

Where I am now as I write this book? I realize that I am somewhere in the middle of being lost and finding my way. For many years, I have had on my heart and in my mind the idea that I needed to change the image of a scientist in the media. I have looked at television and realized that most woman are portrayed as over sexualized, or so nerdy that no one really sees them as being sexy. Women in STEM are usually not looked at as being fashionable or even cute. Why not?

As I looked at this issue and started to work in it, my original dream started to manifest into something else. I realized that as I learn and grow, my dreams and aspirations do the same. It started off with changing the image of women and morphed into the image of all STEM professionals, and even included arts. Science and arts are two programs that are often left behind in primary schools when it comes to learning. All day you are taught to read, associate colors, and understand current events, but things like science and arts are left to maybe an hour a day. And why is that? Science, technology, engineering, arts, and math (STEAM) are constantly around us. If we can teach our youth to recognize STEAM in everything they learn, everything they touch, everything they see, then the fear that they have of it can dissipate. For example, if someone is teaching current events to a classroom of students, what about the current event can you relate to STEAM? Perhaps we are talking about the presidential elections. You can team up with the math teacher and teach statistics at the same time. How do we vote in the primaries, and how are these reporters able to give you percentages of who is winning and by how much? That is math in the form of statistics and can be taught simultaneously! What if you are an English teacher and you are teaching the book 1984 by James Orwell? That book is chopped full with technology. You can talk to your class about the importance and hindrance of the technology mentioned in that book as well as compare it to the technologies of today and how they are important and how they hinder people. You can also break down the technologies and discuss why it is important to understand machines so that you are never over ran by them.

EXTRA

Every time I go somewhere and meet someone new, I ask them if they have a business card. If they don't, don't worry, we live in the age of smartphones! I will ask for your number or your email address really quick!

I am on the way to making my dreams a reality and I will not stop until I get there. The best thing you can do for your child is to support his/her dreams anyway you possibly can. Dreams and innovative ideas that blow STEAM will fuel our lives to places we have never been before!

www.ingramcontent.com/pod-product-compliance
Lightning Source LLC
Chambersburg PA
CBHW051238090426
42742CB00001B/15